Mel Bay's First Lessons

Banjo

by Jack Hatfield

CD Contents

1	Tuning reference	
2	Go Tell Aunt Rhody	14
3	Exercise: Counting Quarter Notes	15
4	The Pinch	16
5	Go Tell Aunt Rhody (with pinches)	16
6	The Eighth Note	17
7	Tom Dooley	17
8	The Alternating Thumb Roll	18
9	Exercise: Changing Strings with the Alternating Thumb Roll	18
10	Exercise: Mixing the Alternating Thumb Roll and the Pinch	18
11	Tom Dooley (with rolls) slow speed	19
12	Tom Dooley (with rolls) medium speed	19
13	The Three Basic Chords	20
14	Exercise: Changing Chords	21
15	Good Night Ladies, slow speed	21
16	Good Night Ladies, medium speed	21
17	Common Slides	22
18	Exercise: The Slide with the Alternating Thumb Roll	22
19	Rests	23
20	Old Time Religion, slow speed	23
21	Old Time Religion, medium speed	23
22	The Forward Roll	24
23	Exercise: Changing Strings and Chords with the Forward Roll	24
24	Cotton-Eyed Joe, slow speed	25
25	Cotton-Eyed Joe, medium speed	25
26	The Hammer-on	26
27	Exercise: The Hammer-on with Rolls	27
28	Cumberland Gap, slow speed	27
29	Cumberland Gap, medium speed	27
30	Forward Roll #2	28
31	The Tag Lick, Exercise: The Tag Lick with Roll Fill Notes	28
32	Exercise: The Tag Lick with Pinch Fill Notes	29
33	Exercise: The Tag Lick with Pickup Notes	29
34	When The Saints Go Marching In, slow speed	29
35	When The Saints Go Marching In, medium speed	29
36	Common Pull-offs	30
37	Exercise: Pull-offs	31
38	Cripple Creek, slow speed	31
39	Cripple Creek, medium speed	31

In the following programs, the rhythm instruments are in the right channel and the banjo is in the left channel.

40	Tom Dooley, performing speed with rhythm	19
41	Good Night Ladies, performing speed with rhythm	21
42	Old Time Religion, performing speed with rhythm	23
43	Cotton-Eyed Joe, performing speed with rhythm	25
44	Cumberland Gap, performing speed with rhythm	27
45	When The Saints Go Marching In, performing speed with rhythm	29
46	Cripple Creek, performing speed with rhythm	31

A Deering Golden Era Banjo was used on this recording.

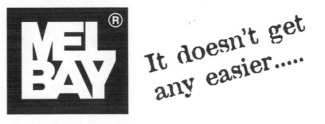

1 2 3 4 5 6 7 8 9 0

Visit us on the Web at www.melbay.com — E-mail us at email@melbay.com

Table of Contents

About this Book 4

About the Author 4

Parts of the Banjo..5

The Picks 6

Tuning the Banjo 7

Holding the Banjo 8

Left Hand Position 9

Right Hand Position 10

How to Read Tablature, an Overview 11

Practice Guidelines..12

Lesson 1 Playing A Simple Melody From Tablature 13
    Using a Metronome, Left-Hand Finger Placement, GO TELL AUNT RHODY 14

Lesson 2 Counting Time 15

Lesson 3 The Pinch, GO TELL AUNT RHODY (with Pinches) 16

Lesson 4 The Eighth Note, TOM DOOLEY 17

Lesson 5 The Roll, The Alternating Thumb Roll 18

Lesson 6 Playing a Song With the Alternating Thumb Roll
    Melody Notes and Fill Notes, TOM DOOLEY (with rolls) 19

Lesson 7 The Three Basic Chords 20
    GOOD NIGHT LADIES, Proper Position Checklist 21

Lesson 8 The Slide 22
    Rests, Pickup Notes, OLD TIME RELIGION 23

Lesson 9 The Forward Roll, Recognizing Rolls by Shape 24
    Licks, COTTON -EYED JOE 25

Lesson 10 The Hammer-On 26
    The E Minor Chord, Caution Marks, Repeat Marks, CUMBERLAND GAP 27

Lesson 11 Forward Roll #2, The Tag Lick..28
    WHEN THE SAINTS GO MARCHING IN 29

Lesson 12 The Pull-Off 30
    CRIPPLE CREEK 31

For Further Study... 32

About This Book

This book is designed to show the person with no musical experience how to play the five-string banjo in the popular three-finger style. Many folks call this style "Scruggs style" after Earl Scruggs, the master musician who refined and popularized it. The three-finger style taught in this book is also known as "bluegrass" style, though many different styles of music can be played using these techniques.

To use this method it is not required that you learn to read music, though the popular convention known as *tablature* is used to communicate all musical examples. Tablature, or "Tab" is a graphic representation that shows you what notes to play, what fingers to use and the duration of each note. Tab is used in virtually all banjo instruction manuals. It is very simple to learn. Most students understand the basic concept and can play music by looking at tab in just a few minutes.

This book will teach you the basic fundamentals of three-finger style and will give you a repertoire of several tunes that are instructive and fun to play. It is very important to listen to the accompanying recording repeatedly and to play along with it, especially if you are using this book as a self-instruction guide. On the recording, the rhythm instruments are isolated in the right channel. After you have learned a tune, you can adjust the balance control of your stereo to the right, eliminating the banjo so you can play along with the band. This is a more enjoyable way to practice, and it insures that you develop good rhythm. When you are ready to play with real live musicians, it will be much easier for you (and for them!) if you have already established good timing by practicing along with the recording.

About the Author

Jack Hatfield is a native of Knoxville, Tennessee. He has been a regular contributor to *Banjo Newsletter* magazine for twenty-five years and has authored several best-selling banjo instruction books by his own publishing company and for Mel Bay Publications, Inc. He has been a faculty member at prestigious banjo seminars such as the *Tennessee Banjo Institute,* the *Maryland Banjo Academy* and the *Nashville Academy of Traditional Music.* Jack is director of *Banjo Newsletter Workshops* which feature top recording artists and other *Banjo Newsletter* columnists. He has performed and taught workshops all over the U.S.A. and the United Kingdom. He has been a finalist at the *National Banjo Championship* at Winfield, Kansas and the Tennessee and Kentucky state banjo championships. He has entertained at venues such as *Dollywood* theme park and the *Dixie Stampede* in Pigeon Forge, Tennessee. Jack currently plays the convention circuit with his band *True Blue* and operates a mail order/e-commerce business called *Hatfield Music,* catering to the needs of banjo players worldwide.

Parts of the Banjo

It is important to learn the parts of the banjo. Several of the parts will be referred to later in this book. Many of the problems beginners face are due partially to improper adjustments such as high strings which make it difficult to note the strings or improper neck relief, which can cause the strings to buzz. Before beginning this course, take your banjo to a qualified repair person and have it checked out. Have new strings installed, and ask to watch so you can do it yourself in the future.

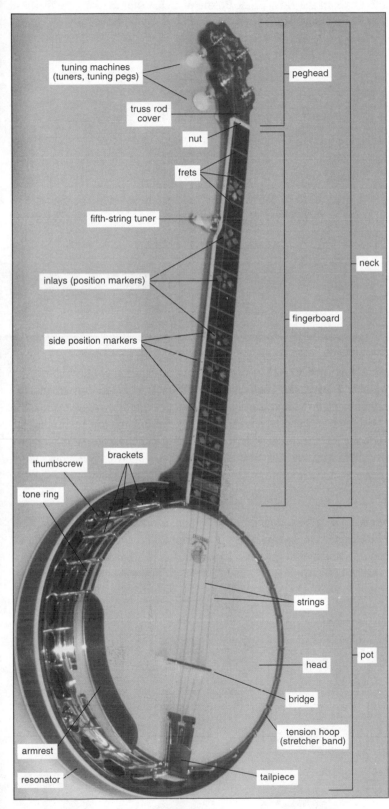

Front View

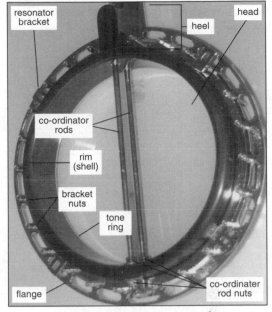

Back view, resonater removed

Adjustments

The amount of bow (relief) in the neck is controlled by adjusting the nut or allen fitting on the end of the *truss rod*, a metal rod running the length of the neck under the fingerboard. It is accessed on most banjos by removing the *truss rod cover* on the peghead.

The *string* height (action) is changed by adjusting the nuts on the top co-ordinater rod on the inside and outside of the rim, near the tailpiece.

The *tailpiece* tension (downward pressure on the strings) can be changed on many banjos by turning a screw on the end of the tailpiece.

The *head* tension is adjusted by adjusting the bracket nuts, which changes the pressure on the *tension hoop*.

The intonation (noting "in-tune" up the neck) can be adjusted by moving the *bridge* in either direction.

The tension on the *tuning machines* can be adjusted using the screw that goes through the middle of the button.

The Picks

In order to produce adequate volume and consistent tone, it is necessary to wear picks on the fingers and thumb of the right hand. Picks may be purchased at practically any stringed instrument dealer. Many beginners have an aversion to using picks, but they eventually realize that producing the desired sound is virtually impossible without them, and they often end up wasting valuable practice time getting used to them later. For this reason, it is best to use picks from the very first day.

Metal finger picks are recommended for the index and middle finger of the right hand. Plastic or nylon thumb picks are the best. The thumb picks generally come in three sizes. Choose a size that fits snugly with little or no discomfort. Though the metal finger picks can be shaped to fit almost any size fingers, extra small finger picks are available for children and small adults.

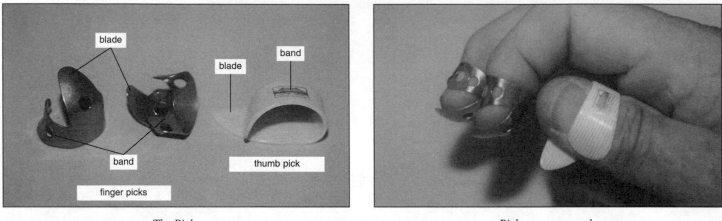

The Picks   *Picks worn properly*

The blade of the finger pick (the part that strikes the string) should be bent back in a uniform curve so that the tip of the blade almost touches the fingernail. Shaping can be accomplished by opening up the band and placing the finger pick over the thumb with the thumbprint on the inside of the blade, then pressing it in a rolling motion against a hard surface. The bands of the finger picks (the parts that go around the finger) should be shaped so that they fit snugly over the fingertip with no flat surfaces which may cause discomfort. The finger picks should be tight enough so they do not move around on the finger, but they should not be so snug as to be uncomfortable. Once the blade of the finger pick is shaped, the band can be shaped with needle nosed pliers to fit the fingertip. The index finger pick will be smaller than the middle finger pick. Wear the same finger pick on the same finger at all times. You may want to mark the picks with nail polish or a scratch so you can identify them easily.

Though one of the three sizes of thumb picks will fit most thumbs, it may occasionally be necessary to shape the thumb pick. This can be accomplished by holding the blade with pliers or tongs and dipping the band in hot water. Tap water will not be hot enough. It will be necessary to heat the water using a stove or microwave oven. Never heat a pick with a match or open flame. Most are made of a very volatile material that will explode into an extremely hot flame unexpectedly. Personal injury and damage to furniture or floors may occur.

Shaping the finger picks   *Shaping the thumb pick*

Tuning the Banjo

It is recommended that you tune the banjo using an electronic tuner. This will put the banjo in *standard* or *concert* pitch. Use the tuner before every practice session. In time your ear will become accustomed to the "in tune" sound and you will notice when the banjo is out of tune. If you tune with an electronic tuner, the banjo will be in tune with the practice recording that accompanies this book. Below are the letter name of the notes to select when using the electronic tuner.

First string:	**D**
Second string:	**B**
Third string:	**G**
Fourth string:	**D, one octave below the first string**
Fifth String:	**G, one octave above the third string**

If you already have a well developed ear because of prior experiences in music, you may be able to tune the open strings "by ear." If an electronic tuner is not available, there are reference tuning notes at the beginning of the recording that accompanies this book. If an electronic tuner or stereo is not available, you may use the following method to tune the banjo strings relative to each other, though the entire banjo may be higher or lower than "standard" pitch. This is fine for playing unaccompanied. It is only when playing with other musicians or a recording that tuning at standard pitch is critical.

Note: Count the strings from the bottom. The bottom string (the one closest to the floor) is the *first string*. The second string from the bottom is the *second string,* and so on.

Play the open first string (*open* means without fretting it with the left hand).

Place any fingertip on the second string, just behind the third fret (on the peghead side of the fret). Play the open first string and then play the fretted second string.

Compare these two notes. If the banjo is in tune, they will sound identical. If the second string/third fret note is lower in pitch than the note on the first string/open, tighten the second string tuning machine slightly and compare again. If the second string/third fret note is higher in pitch than the first string/open, loosen the second string tuning machine slightly and compare again. Continue this procedure until the second string/third fret note is exactly the same pitch as the first string/open note.

Now we will use the "in tune" second string to adjust the pitch of the third string. Hold down the third string behind the fourth fret. Compare this note to the second string/open. Adjust the third string tuning machine as above until the pitch of the two notes sounds identical.

Now we will use the "in tune" third string to adjust the pitch of the fourth string. Hold the fourth string down just behind the fifth fret. Compare this note to the third string/open. Adjust the fourth string tuning machine until the two notes are at the same pitch.

Now for the fifth string. Hold down the first string just behind the fifth fret. Compare this note to the fifth string/open. Adjust the fifth string tuning machine until the two notes are the same.

Tuning Notes:

Worn strings will not tune properly. Strings are often too old to tune properly before any corrosion is visible. Change strings every thirty to forty hours of playing time or whenever tuning becomes a problem. Wiping the strings after every practice session can double their life.

The bridge placement also affects tuning. A banjo dealer can adjust the bridge placement for you. Basically, the distance from the nut to the twelfth fret should be the same as the distance from the twelfth fret to the bridge. In other words, the twelfth fret is the midpoint of the vibrating string.

Changing the tension on the strings may slightly pull the neck off center, slightly altering the pitch of some of the strings already tuned. Therefore, it will usually be necessary to repeat the entire procedure at least once to "fine tune" the banjo. Below is the tuning procedure again, abbreviated.

Open first string = Second string, third fret
Open second string = Third string, fourth fret
Open third string = Fourth string, fifth fret
Open fifth string = First string, fifth fret

Holding The Banjo

Sitting Position (recommended)   *Standing Position*

It is recommended that you practice while in a sitting position. Not only will fatigue be less of a factor, but the left hand will be free to move around the fingerboard more easily. The use of a stool, easy chair or couch is not recommended. Sit *with good posture* in a straight back chair which has no arms. Place the soles of both feet squarely on the floor. If your feet do not touch the floor, find a smaller chair. The banjo should rest in the lap, centered between the legs, so gravity and friction is utilized to support it in an upright position. This will minimize the effort from your arms and hands, which must be free to note the strings. Do not prop the banjo up on one leg. Hold the neck between a forty degree angle and a sixty degree angle relative to the floor.

It is highly recommended that a strap be used, even though sitting down. The use of the strap plus the weight of your right forearm on the armrest will keep neck of the banjo from dropping to a more horizontal angle, making it more difficult to note properly. This is especially true of cheaper lightweight banjos. Adjust the strap so that it supports some of the weight of the banjo. The banjo should be maintained at the proper angle by the contact with the upper legs, the weight of the right arm, the left hand under the banjo neck, and the strap. Later when you are ready to jam or perform for others, you may wish to practice while standing. Take care that the strap is adjusted while in a sitting position as described above. If the strap is adjusted to the proper length, there will be no change in the position of the banjo relative to the body when going from a sitting position to a standing position.

Remember… *always* practice proper posture whether sitting or standing. Resist the urge to crane your neck over the banjo to look at the fingerboard. Use the position markers on the side of the neck to locate the intended frets instead of sticking your neck out to see the inlays on the fingerboard.

If you practice with proper position and use a straight back chair, you will not only be able to play more efficiently and without getting tired as quickly, you will also be more relaxed and confident.

Left Hand Position

There are two primary goals in learning proper left hand position. The first is that only the *tips* of the fingers touch the strings. The second is realizing fast and efficient movement up and down the neck. In order to position the left hand properly, follow these steps:

1) Lay your left hand down on your knee with the palm facing upward.

2) TOTALLY RELAX the hand. The fingers are curved, the hand forming a cupped or "C" shape.

3) Close up your thumb so that a "V" is formed by the third joint of the thumb and the first index finger joint, where the index finger joins the hand.

4) Bend the elbow to raise your left arm so that the hand cradles the banjo neck. The neck rests lightly in the "V" and the thumb is in the area behind the first fret. Maintain the relaxed state.

5) Arch the wrist slightly away from you. This should position the fingertips less than an inch from the fingerboard and keep the palm from touching the neck.

When noting a string, only the *tip* of the finger touches the string. No part of the finger should touch the adjacent strings. It is very important to keep the fingernails trimmed short. The banjo pot should be perpendicular to the floor. A slumping posture will allow the banjo to tilt back, making it more difficult to note the strings with the fingertips. Maintain a state of relaxed alertness at all times. Practically no muscles in the fingers or hand should be used unless actually noting a string. Use only enough force to obtain a clear tone with no muted or buzzing sounds. *Do not allow your palm to touch the neck.*

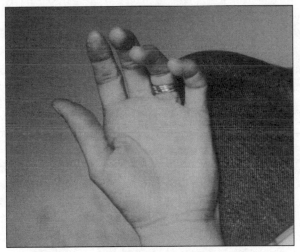

Hand on knee, relaxed

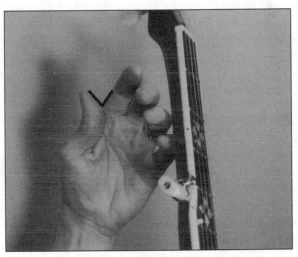

Forming a "V", hand behind neck

Player's point of view

View from front

Right Hand Position

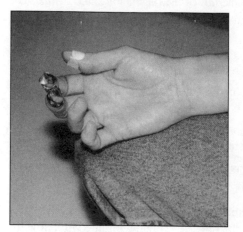

Right hand, relaxed

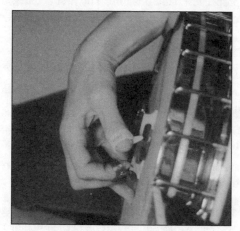

Right hand, player's view

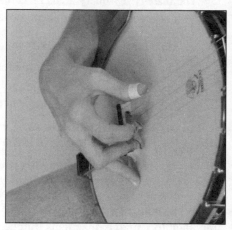

Right hand, front view

Place the inside of the right forearm on the armrest. Do not use any muscles in the arm. Let the natural force of gravity hold the right forearm firmly against the armrest. Anchor the ring and little fingers of the right hand on the head so that the middle finger contacts the strings about one inch from the bridge. Later you will learn to alter the right hand placement for tonal variation. The two anchored fingers plus the forearm on the armrest creates a three point support, the most stable system possible. A two-legged stool falls over. A four-legged stool can rock if all legs are not exactly the same length. However, even with legs of different lengths, a three legged stool will remain stable.

Many people have difficulty keeping the ring finger down, especially when the middle finger moves to strike the string. Be patient... if after a couple of weeks you cannot keep the ring finger anchored, you may want to intentionally raise the little finger so the ring finger is forced by the weight of the arm to remain on the head of the banjo. After the ring finger is trained to stay down the little finger can easily be replaced. Try this experiment at least a month before giving up. A small percentage of students have extreme difficulty keeping the ring finger down. If after several weeks of effort you cannot keep the ring finger down, do not worry about it. You can still become an accomplished banjo player. You may be able to train the ring finger to stay down later.

It is best to keep the ring and little finger straight, but some people have great difficulty keeping the ring finger straight while striking a string with the middle finger. If you are one of these people, curl the ring and little finger so the side of the knuckle and the edge of the fingernail touches the head. If you cannot keep the ring finger down at all and the right hand moves as you play, you may have to use a little muscle pressure, forcing the forearm to anchor more solidly on the armrest. The main thing is that the right hand does not rock as you play. The hand should remain completely steady. Only the fingers should move, mostly from the second knuckle and somewhat less from the first knuckle. The thumb should move almost entirely from the first joint, where it joins the hand. The picking motion should be relaxed and fluid. Do not jerk the fingers. Keep the picking fingers in a relaxed curve, with the tips of the picks within three-quarters of an inch from the strings at all times. Efficiency of motion will produce more speed and better tone. The tips of the picks should travel no more than one eighth inch below the string. To check pick depth, align your eye with the plane of the strings and notice how far below the string the picks travel. The more lightly you pick, the easier it is to control the depth of the picks. Many motion-related and fatigue problems are the result of trying to pick with too much force. Force can be altered later for melody emphasis and tone control. For now, simply try to find a consistent attack that is comfortable and efficient.

The wrist should be slightly arched so that the thumb can pick down on the strings (toward the head) instead of across the strings (toward the floor). A fuller, louder tone is produced by picking in a downward motion. Bending the finger picks back almost to the fingernails will help you to set the strings oscillating in a direction which is perpendicular to the plane of the banjo head.

How To Read Tablature – An Overview

Tablature (*tab* for short) is a method of writing music for stringed instruments that shows what notes to play graphically instead of by standard musical notation. With tablature there is no memorizing of note names as there is in standard musical notation. Tablature will be explained in more detail as the book progresses, but it would be helpful to have a general understanding now.

Here is how it works: Banjo tablature consists of five lines. Each line represents one of the banjo strings. The first (top) line represents the first (bottom) string of the banjo. The second line of tablature represents the second (from the bottom) banjo string, and so on. It's exactly like holding the banjo in your lap with the head facing upward and looking down at the strings.

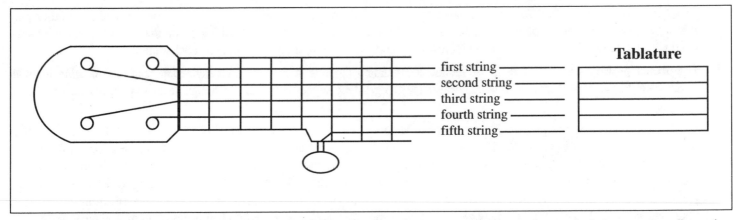

The numbers located on the lines indicate at which fret to note the string. A zero on a line means to pluck the corresponding string *open* (without fretting it with the left hand). The letters above and below the number indicate which finger to use.

A zero means to play the corresponding string "open" (no left hand finger):

Play the third string, open

Numbers on the lines indicate which fret to hold the finger behind on that string:

Play the second string, third fret

A capital letter under the note tells you which right hand finger to use:

T = Right Thumb
I = Right Index finger
M = Right Middle finger

A lower case letter above the note shows which left hand finger to use:

i = Left index finger
m = Left middle finger
r = Left ring finger
p = Left pinky (little finger)

In the example below, hold your fingertip behind the second fret on the fourth string.

Use the middle finger to note the string
and the right thumb to pluck it.

The duration of each note is indicated by marks known as *stems*, *beams* and *flags* which are attached to the fret number. There are also symbols called *rests* that indicate pauses. These features will be explained later as you need them.

Practice Guidelines

Anybody who *really* wants to learn a musical instrument can do so. If you have a burning desire to learn, you will eventually be successful even in spite of poor practice habits. But why do it the hard way? Develop good practice habits early and you will progress more quickly.

1) **Practice EVERY DAY.** As a beginner, thirty minutes per day is a realistic goal. An hour per day divided into two thirty minute sessions is *more than* twice as productive. Make the practice session a daily regimen, like brushing your teeth. Try to practice at the same time every day, in the same place. If you must skip a day or two, try to make up by practicing extra the next few days. If you cannot commit to a minimum of a half hour practice per day, do not even consider learning to play!

2) **Practice without distraction.** You cannot realize the full benefit from your practice time if you have the television on, children playing in the room, other music playing, or any other distraction. Choose a time of day and a location that provides an environment conducive to study...the earlier the better so you will be alert. A bedroom, study or basement room is ideal.

3) **Use proper position.** Pages 6 - 8 demonstrate how to sit and how to hold the banjo. Too many people read this one time and within days are practicing with poor technique because they forget these suggestions. Poor technique leads to poor results, extra effort and wasted time.

4) **Use the recording.** A carpenter would never think of building a house without a blueprint. This is an aural art. Use the "song blueprint" which accompanies this book. The amount of time that it takes to learn a tune may be cut *by as much as half* if the essence of the tune is in your head before you ever attempt to learn from the tablature. Listen to the recording as you drive or work around the house. Even semi-conscious listening will speed up your learning time considerably. Use the recording to check your progress, playing along with the slow version until you are synchronized with it. *Then* move on to the next level. After learning a tune, adjust your balance control to the right and play along with the band. This instills good rhythm and is more fun than playing alone.

5) **PLAY SLOWLY!** Learning music is much more efficient if it is done slowly and correctly the first time. It may not sound like banjo music until weeks later when your speed has increased, but valuable time will not be wasted going back to correct errors. Play so slowly that the spacing of the beats is uniform from the first time you play it. There should be no buzzing or muted notes.

6) **Memorize the tunes.** Tablature is a wonderful tool, but many students rely on it too long. If you continue to play from the printed page your playing will sound mechanical. To give your music character and to focus on the finer points of technique, you *must* play from memory. Some of the earlier tunes may be discarded later as your repertoire increases, but a few key tunes should be retained. This is how speed is developed; naturally, from hundreds of repetitions over time.

It is best to memorize in phrases. Most banjo music consists of musical phrases with a definite beginning and ending. Recognizing these phrases reduces the time it takes to memorize a tune. You do not speak in alphabet letters...you speak in words and sentences. Music is played the same way. Once a tune is memorized, learn to focus not on the individual notes, but to interpret your music in phrases like it is sung. It will not only be easier to memorize, it will also sound less mechanical. Look for repetition. Most tunes contain phrases which are repeated exactly or very similarly. If you recognize a repeated phrase you will not waste time re-memorizing it.

7) **About young children:** If the student is a child under ten or eleven years old, the parent should be willing to make the commitment of practicing with the child *daily*. Most children beyond the age of five or six have the physical ability to play, but generally lack the attention span to practice thirty minutes daily unless a sibling, parent or other adult plays alongside them, making it more fun. Two fifteen-minute sessions per day is recommended for kids instead of a single thirty-minute session.

Suggested Daily Practice Routine

Five minutes: Warmup. Just as an athlete must warm up and stretch before an event, the musician should loosen up the fingers and get the mind in gear. Play rolls, exercises and simple tunes you have already mastered at a medium to slow tempo with the recording or a metronome if possible.

Ten minutes: Exercises and problem areas. Identify the areas that are giving you trouble. Extract the two or four measure phrase that contains the problem spot an play it repeatedly with the recording or a metronome. Play the entire phrase, not just the two or three notes that you are having difficulty with. If you are having trouble with a certain technique such as a pull-off or slide, play an exercise that focuses only on that technique. *Play so slowly it is absolutely error-free.*

Ten minutes: Work on the newest lesson and on memorizing the two or three previous lessons. Keep it slow and read all the accompanying text every day.

Five minutes: Play for fun! The work is over... now just do whatever you feel like. You will be enjoying the banjo so much you will probably extend the session without even realizing it.

This is a typical thirty minute practice schedule. For a one hour session, simply double the time devoted to each segment of the practice session. However, two thirty-minute sessions per day may be more effective than a single one-hour session for the first few days or weeks.

Lesson 1 – Playing A Simple Melody From Tablature

First we will explore tablature and get the fingers loosened up by playing some simple tunes you probably know from childhood. Though these tunes may seem boring and childish to some, they will be learned very fast because they are already "in your head". You will know immediately if you are making an error. Later we will play a more advanced version of these tunes and learn some real banjo standards.

In tablature, the lines represent the five strings of the banjo. The first string, (the bottom string, closest to the floor) is represented by the *top* line of tablature. If you see a zero on the line, play the corresponding string *open,* which means "without holding a left-hand finger on it":

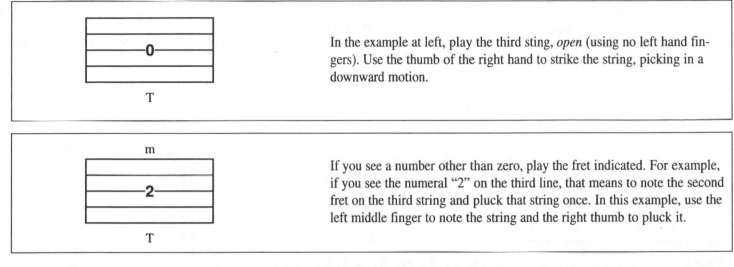

In the example at left, play the third sting, *open* (using no left hand fingers). Use the thumb of the right hand to strike the string, picking in a downward motion.

If you see a number other than zero, play the fret indicated. For example, if you see the numeral "2" on the third line, that means to note the second fret on the third string and pluck that string once. In this example, use the left middle finger to note the string and the right thumb to pluck it.

In the following song, be sure to follow the left hand fingering marked above the tab. When a fretted note is to be repeated do not pick up the finger only to put it back down again immediately. If a note is to be played on the same string but at a different fret, simply relax the pressure a little and slide the finger from one fret position to the next without actually lifting the fingertip from the string. This will increase speed and accuracy and avoid the "choppy" sound created when the string stops vibrating suddenly. Be sure the left hand finger contacts the string just behind the fret. All strokes of the the right hand thumb should be in a downward motion, towards the floor. The fingers strike only in an upward direction. The vertical lines in the tab will help you keep your place, but they have nothing to do with the note spacing. Do not pause at vertical lines or when repeating the song.

Notice your left hand position. Be sure to form a "V"shape by closing your thumb up to your index finger knuckle. Arch the left wrist away from you so only the tips of the fingers contact the strings. Remember, *the palm of the left hand should not touch the back of the banjo neck.*

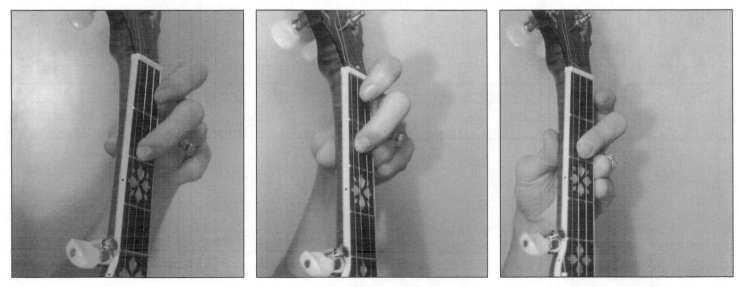

Correct noting of string   *Incorrect!*
Fingertip too far back   *Incorrect! Finger flat,*
touching adjacent string

13

Using a Metronome

Eventually you will develop a more acute sense of rhythm, but at first it is a good idea to use a metronome or rhythm recording like the one that accompanies this book to provide an external rhythm source. This will train your internal clock, instilling good rhythm at an early stage in your development. Set the metronome at whatever speed you can play all notes within the tune perfectly, no matter how slowly. At first try a metronome setting of sixty to seventy beats per minute. When you can play the tune perfectly several times through, increase the speed of the metronome by five or ten beats per minute. When you have reached about 100 beats per minute, you may proceed to the next lesson. If you do not have a metronome, play along with the recording. If tapping your foot comes naturally, that is great. If not, do not try to force it. Concentrate on the notes and synchronizing them with the recording or the metronome instead of thinking about your foot.

Left hand Finger Placement

When you note a string with the left hand, be sure to place the very tip of your finger just behind the fret. If you hear a dull or muted sound, the fingertip is either protruding over the fret or a finger placed on an adjacent string is touching the muted string. Do not use too much force. This will slow you down and cause premature fatigue. Use only enough pressure so that a clear tone with no buzzing sound is produced. If you hear a buzzing sound, you are either not using enough pressure or your fingertip is too far behind the fret. Remember, the suggested left hand finger is shown in lower case letters above each note. The letter "p" ("pinky") is used for the little finger because the letter "l" may be easily confused with the letter "i".

In the following arrangement, the vertical lines create boxes. Each of these boxes represents a unit of time. If you are playing with a metronome or tapping your foot, play the contents of one box on each metronome click or foot tap. When there is an empty box, play no note but leave a space equal to the time allotted for all the other boxes. In other words, allow the metronome to click once before proceeding to the contents of the next box. We will discuss timing in detail in the next lesson, but for now this will suffice. If you simply play along with the demonstration recording your note spacing will be correct. Remember to listen to the recording just before playing each melody, and be able to hum or whistle the tune by memory before you even try to play it on the banjo.

Go Tell Aunt Rhody

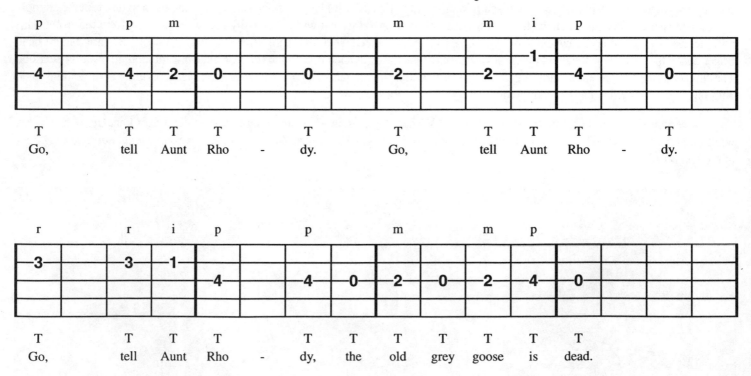

14

Lesson 2 – Counting Time

A *beat* is a unit of time. All beats within a song are of equal duration. Think of a heartbeat or the ticking of a clock. As you play a song, this internal "clock" is always ticking inside you.

A *measure* or *bar* is a grouping of beats. There will be a vertical line called a *measure line* or *bar line* dividing the measures. Within a song, there is an equal number of beats in each measure. It is easier to keep your place in a song if you view the tablature in entire measures instead of by individual beats. It's like counting to a hundred by "tens" instead of by ones: It's easier to say "ten, twenty, thirty, forty..."etc. than to say "one, two three, four, five, six..."etc.

The most popular grouping or *meter* is called *4/4 time* (pronounced "four-four time"). It is also known as *common time* because the overwhelming majority of Western music is written in this meter. The other popular meter is *3/4 time,* in which there are three beats per measure. It is also known as *waltz time.* However, all the music in this book is written in 4/4 time.

A *quarter note* is a note that lasts one full beat. It is called a "quarter note" because in 4/4 time it is a note that consumes a quarter of a measure. In tablature, a quarter note will be indicated by a vertical stem below the note.

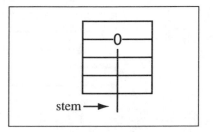

stem ⟶

Quarter Note

To count quarter notes, count as you play with the metronome or recording; "One two three four, One two three four..."etc. Say the count precisely as you play each note. The count, the metronome click and the note should all occur simultaneously. Emphasize the first beat of each measure. Say it *and* play it more loudly than the other beats: "**One** two three four, **One** two three four..."etc. This helps you keep your place, emphasizes the important melody notes and gives the music a pleasant rhythmic surge. Set your metronome at a slow speed or practice along with the recording as you count and play the quarter notes below. As with all the exercises and tunes in this book, repeat several times without pausing when you start over at the beginning.

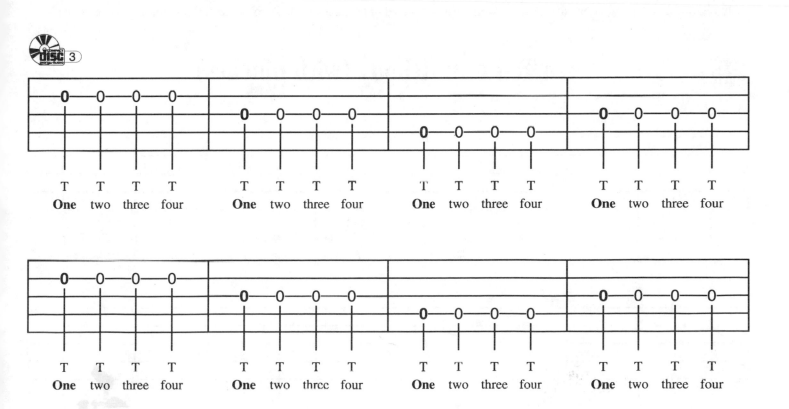

Lesson Three – The Pinch

Playing music is like speaking or singing. We do not ramble on incessantly when we speak. We must stop to breathe. Also, our words must be organized into groups that make sense to the listener. Therefore, we speak in sentences. Within sentences there are smaller phrases. We punctuate our speaking with emphasis on certain syllables and by pauses of varying lengths. These pauses are represented by commas, periods and other punctuation marks.

Banjo players must also have punctuation marks that will help them define the musical phrases. The *Pinch* is the most basic of these devices. Pinches are like commas and periods in our musical "sentences". The pinch fills up space without detracting from the melody. It usually signals the end of a musical phrase. The amount of emphasis (right hand force) and the length of the pinch varies according to the melody being interpreted. It may be a single pinch, like a musical "comma," or it may be a double pinch (a four-beat figure). The double pinch is more finite, like a period at the end of a sentence. The first note of the double pinch is usually the last important melody note of a phrase. The pinch is performed by playing two notes simultaneously, usually on the open first and fifth strings. It will be shown in tablature as two notes on one timing stem with a "P" underneath.

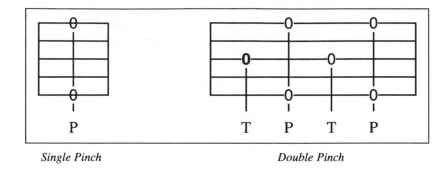

Single Pinch   *Double Pinch*

Now we will play a familiar melody using timing stems and pinches. Remember to position your left thumb on the back of the neck in the area behind the first fret and leave it there throughout the song. You should be able to reach all notes without moving your thumb from this position.

Be sure the left wrist is arched *away* from the body and the the palm is not touching the neck. Are the very tips of the fingers contacting the strings? Are you noting the strings just behind the frets, not on top of or midway between the frets? Is each finger touching only one string, not the adjacent string? If the string makes a muted or buzzing sound, one or more of these mistakes is being made.

Go Tell Aunt Rhody (with pinches)

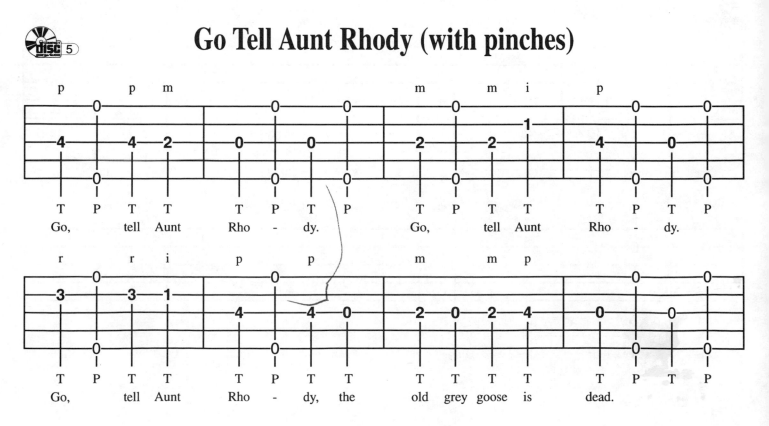

Lesson Four – The Eighth Note

An *eighth note* is a note that lasts a half beat (it is an eighth of a measure in 4/4 time). Therefore, two eighth notes consume the same amount of time as one quarter note. The eighth note is attached to one or more other eighth notes by a heavy horizontal line known as a *beam*. The eighth notes will usually come in groups of two or four, but this has no bearing on the duration of the note.

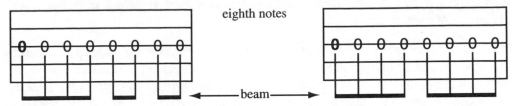

eighth notes

←—— beam ——→

To count eighth notes, say the number of the count *("one", "two", "three"* or *"four")* on the first half of the beat, and the word *"and"* (&) on the second half of the beat. Set your metronome at a slow speed or practice along with the recording as you count and play the eighth notes below:

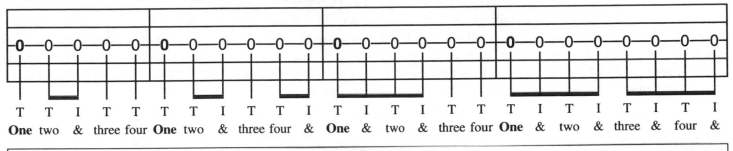

Alternating Right Hand Fingers

Note that in the examples above, *the same right hand finger is never repeated after an eighth note.* This is a basic principle of three finger banjo. Doing so may seem easy enough now, but will cause irregular note spacing later as your speed increases. Alternating right hand fingers is one of the secrets of playing fast.

Now let us play a song using eighth notes. The old folk song *Tom Dooley* should be familiar enough to most folks. If you are not familiar with it, listen to the recording so many times that you can hum or whistle it by memory before learning the arrangement below.

Remember to look for repetition. The first measure is similar to the third measure. The third measure is identical to the fifth measure. The right hand sequence in measures two, four, six and eight is the same. Recognizing repetition when you first begin working on a new song will speed your learning immensely. You will also begin to think in musical phrases instead of individual notes, a primary goal we will discuss again later.

Tom Dooley

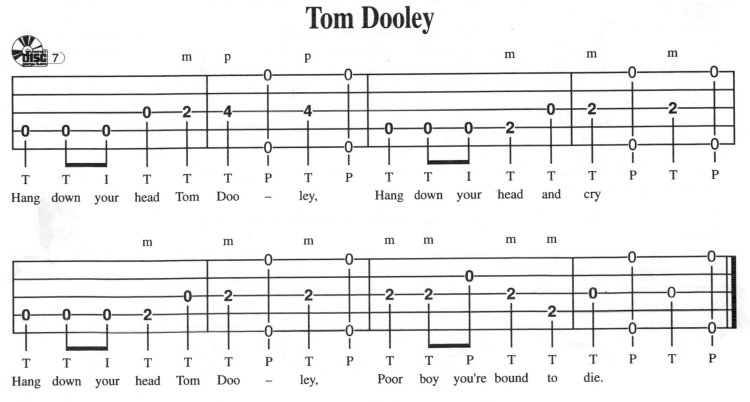

17

Lesson Five – The Roll

Three-finger banjo players often play amazingly fast. An experienced banjo player may play as many as *fourteen notes a second* on some tunes. How could anybody possibly think that fast? The answer is that banjo players learn to think in groups of notes instead of individual notes. These note groups are called *rolls*. Banjo players practice a four-note or eight-note finger sequence until they can play it automatically without thinking of the individual notes. If you repeat a finger sequence enough times, you reach the point that you can do it with one thought instead of many thoughts.

When we speak, we do not speak in alphabet letters. We speak, read and write in words made up of alphabet letters. The individual notes are like the alphabet letters and the rolls are like words. Because of the different roll combinations and left hand options, an incredible number of different melodies can be played with just a few rolls. Almost all Scruggs style banjo arrangements are composed of only four or five basic finger sequences played in different combinations. Remember, it is the right hand *finger sequence* that defines the roll, not the order of the strings or anything the left hand does. When you learn a roll, you are memorizing the *sequence in which the fingers pick the strings.*

The Alternating Thumb Roll

The easiest and most useful roll is the *Alternating Thumb roll.* As it's name suggests, it requires the use of the thumb every other note. The most popular Alternating Thumb roll is **T I T M,** shown below in tab. Practice it over and over for several minutes until you can do it without thinking. Maintain an equal amount of time between each note, even when starting the roll over. A good test to determine whether you have mastered the roll is to talk while performing it without making any errors. When you can do this, you are ready to use it in a song. Remember, it is *very important* to maintain an equal amount of time between each note.

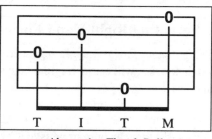

Alternating Thumb Roll

Now let's practice changing strings while playing the Alternating Thumb roll. Repeat the following exercise for five minutes without stopping, maintaining an equal amount of space between each note.

Exercise: Changing Strings With The Alternating Thumb Roll

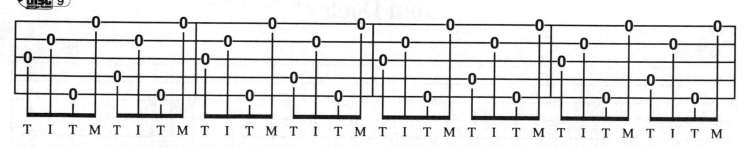

The exercise below will help you learn to mix the Alternating Thumb roll and the pinch. Play it over and over without hesitation along with a metronome or the practice recording.

Exercise: Mixing the Alternating Thumb Roll and the Pinch

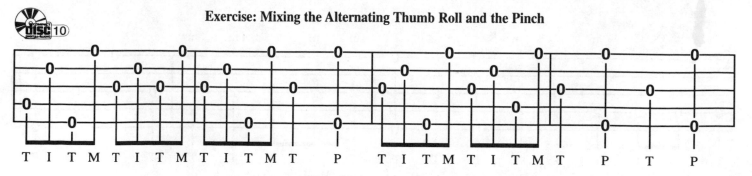

18

Lesson Six – Playing A Song with the Alternating Thumb Roll

Now that you have mastered the Alternating Thumb roll, let's incorporate it into a tune. Songs are much easier to learn if the melody is already familiar. This is why the first tunes in this book were common children's songs. Even if the songs are familiar to you, listen to the recording many times before learning the tab. There are many notes in banjo music that are not in the vocal melody.

Melody Notes and Fill Notes

Not all the notes in a banjo arrangement are of equal importance. In order to maintain the constant flow of notes which is required for the "banjo sound," many *fill notes* will be inserted between the *melody notes*. Melody notes are notes that you would sing a word or syllable on if singing the song. *Fill notes* simply fill up space. They harmonize with the melody notes, but are not notes on which you would sing a word. In this book, the melody notes will be in **bold face type.** Be sure to play them more loudly than the fill notes, which will be in plain type.

Notice that the first beat in each measure is almost always a melody note. This is true in almost all Western music. Therefore, if you develop the habit of emphasizing the first beat of each measure regardless of the string or fret played, the melody will be more apparent in your playing.

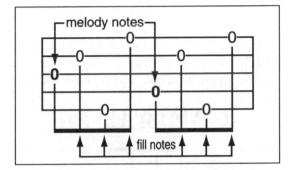

Note that not all the melody notes will be included. As stated, it is very important in three-finger banjo style to maintain a steady unbroken flow of notes. It is even acceptable for the banjo player to omit some melody notes so that this steady flow of notes can be maintained. If the banjo player plays the correct melody note on the first beat of the measure and any other melody notes that will fit into the roll pattern selected, that is usually adequate. The listener's mind will "fill in" most missing melody notes. Compare the banjo roll arrangement of *Tom Dooley* below with the single note melody on page 17. All the important melody notes are included, but there are some words and syllables in the lyrics that are not represented by melody notes in the roll version below.

Tom Dooley (with rolls)

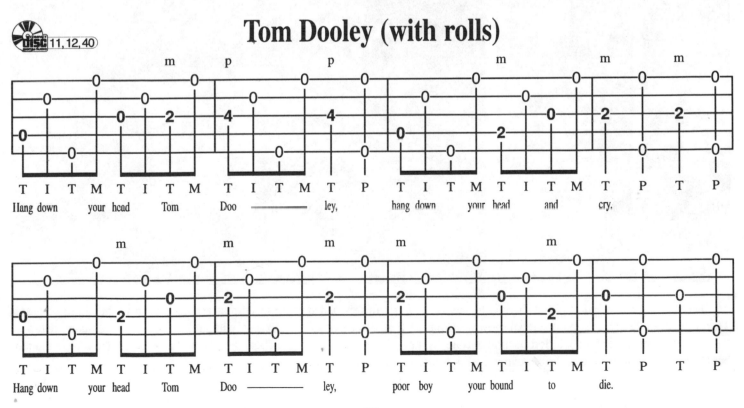

19

Lesson 7 – The Three Basic Chords

A *chord* is a group of several notes that have a pleasant sound when played together. Notes in a chord may be played simultaneously as in a strum or they may be played in sequence, which is the way banjo players commonly us them in a solo or "lead" arrangement.

The *chord diagram* is a graphic representation used to show how to form chords. In the chord diagram, the vertical lines represent the strings and the horizontal lines represent the frets. Imagine you are holding the banjo in front of you in a vertical position and looking at the area including the nut and the first few frets. The heavy horizontal line at the top represents the nut. Just as in the tablature, the left hand finger is represented by the letters *i, m, r,* or *p.* To read a chord diagram, simply place the finger that is indicated behind the fret that is indicated, as shown in the photos below.

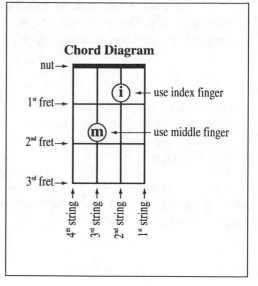

The chord diagrams below show the G Major, C Major and D7 chords, the three basic chords in the key of G Major. This is the most common key for banjo players. Thousands of country, gospel, folk and bluegrass songs can be played using only these three basic chords. Note that because the banjo is already tuned to "open" G tuning, the G Major chord requires no left hand fingers.

In common usage, if there is no other identifying character after the chord symbol, a chord is understood to be a "Major" chord. So, if you see the symbol G, that means "G Major". The other basic chord type we will see later is the *minor* chord, designated by a lower case "m" after the chord symbol. The symbol *Gm* means "G minor." The symbol *G7* means "G Seventh."

G Major Chord   C Major Chord   D7 Chord

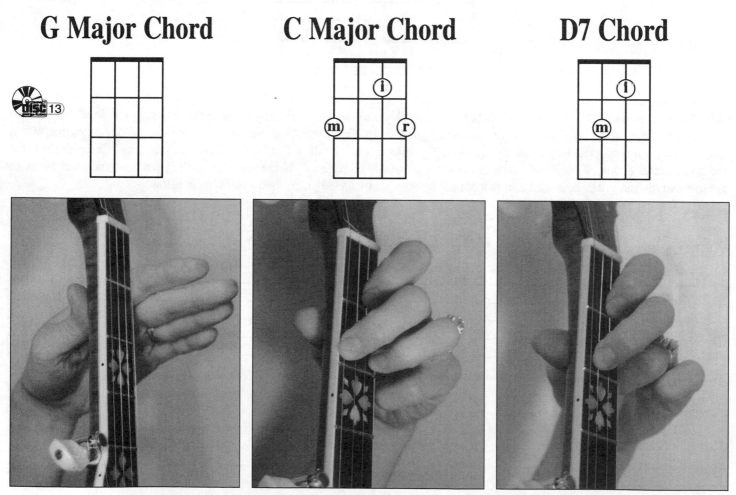

The tab will often indicate that there is to be one or more fingers added or removed that are not shown in the chord diagram. Therefore, even though the chord symbol shown above the tab may not always agree exactly with all the notes in the tablature below, it will give you general hints about left hand fingering. As a rule, hold down the entire chord shown by the chord symbol above the tab, but alter it as you go by adding or removing fingers wherever the tab indicates.

Exercise: Changing Chords

Play the exercise below repeatedly for several minutes with a metronome or the demonstration recording. Make sure each fingertip touches only the intended string, not the adjacent strings. Left hand position is extremely important when playing chords. Be sure the wrist is arched outward and the palm does not touch the back of the neck.

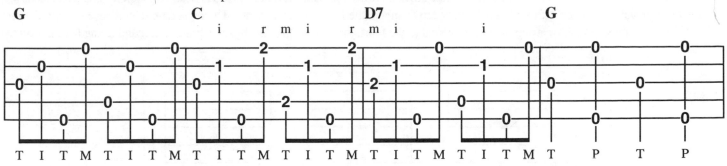

Now we will learn a new song using chords. Note that in the arrangement of *Good Night Ladies* below, the fourth string is not noted when playing the C chord. This does *not* mean it is acceptable to use the middle finger on the first string. Form the full chord as learned previously. Be careful not to touch the third string with the middle finger. After the song is fairly well learned, work on emphasis as a final touch. Strike the bold face notes harder in order to make the melody obvious.

Good Night Ladies

Proper Position Checklist

After playing a few days or weeks, it is easy to forget some of the principles discussed earlier. *Every time* you play a song or exercise, go through the following checklist.

Are you sitting in a straight back chair?
Are you using a strap?
Is your back straight? Do not crane your neck to look over the fingerboard.
Is your right arm relaxed? Use only the muscles in the fingers.
Are the ring and little fingers of the right hand anchored on the head?
Are you using only the *tips* of the picks? The picks should not strike the head of the banjo.
Are both wrists arched, both hands cupped into a "C" shape?
Are fingertips of both hands close to the strings even when not noting a string?
Are you forming a "V" with the left thumb and the base of the index finger?
Is the banjo neck held at a 40 to 60 degree angle to the floor?

Lesson 8 – The Slide

Banjo players use several techniques to make melody notes stand out from fill notes. One of the most effective is the *slide*. The slide is a left hand technique that creates a slurring sound from one note to another. The ending note is usually a melody note. The slide will be shown in tablature as two notes with a dash between them and the letter "s" underneath. The most common slides are from the second to the third fret on the third string, from the second to the fourth fret on the third string, and from the second to the fifth fret on the fourth string:

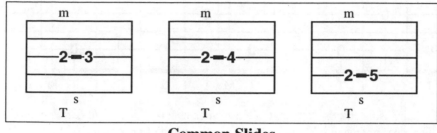

Common Slides

The slide will commonly be incorporated into a roll. When this occurs, the second note of the slide can be on the same timing stem as the next note in the roll. *This does not affect the right hand note spacing.* Maintain an equal space between all eighth notes produced by the right hand, just as you would when there is no slide involved. At beginner speed the slide will usually end before you strike the following note. However, as your speed increases your right hand notes will be closer together and the second note of the slide will become more synchronized with the following note. There is no need at this point to consciously try to synchronize the second note of the slide with the following note in the roll. Simply play along with the recording and try to match the notes exactly.

For slides that begin at the second fret, use the middle finger of your left hand. Keep your left hand thumb in place on the back of the neck. The slide motion is the same motion as snapping the fingers...the middle finger moves from the tip of the thumb to the base of the thumb, with the banjo neck held in between. *Do not* move your hand on the back of the neck. This will get your left hand out of position and can cause you to miss when aiming the finger for the next series of notes. Maintain a hand position with the left thumb in the area behind the first fret. If you have proper left hand position, it should be possible to perform all the slides in this book without moving your thumb. If you are an adult or older child you should be able to slide all the way to the fifth fret with your middle finger without ever moving your left thumb.

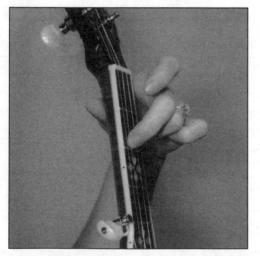

The 2 - 4 Slide, starting position

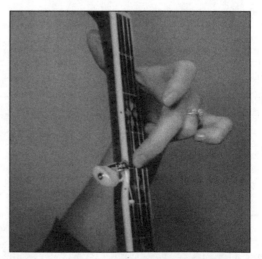

The 2 - 4 Slide, completed

Exercise: The Slide with the Alternating Thumb Roll

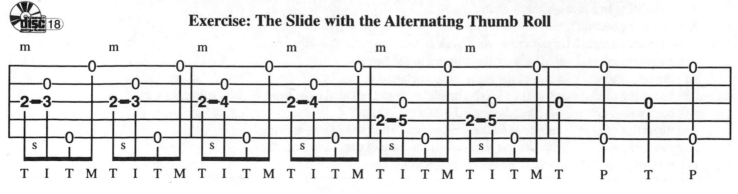

22

Rests

To show a period of silence in the music, a symbol known as the *rest* will be used. A *quarter rest* signifies one full beat of silence. A *half rest* signifies two full beats of silence. Count the beat or beats consumed by the rest but do not play a note or let the previous note ring during these beats. There are other types of rests, but the only ones used in this book are the quarter rest and the half

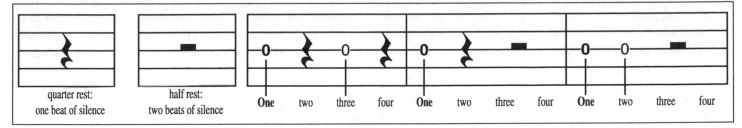

Pickup Notes

Banjo players need a way of signaling to other musicians how fast a tune is to be played and when the rhythm players should start. In order to do this we use *pickup notes*. Pickup notes will usually appear in tab as a partial measure before the first full measure. The last partial measure of the song and the first (pickup) measure added together equal the same number of beats as any other full measure (four beats in 4/4 time or three beats in 3/4 time). The rhythm instruments recognize the pickup notes and all begin together on the first beat of the first full measure. So, pickup notes are like a musical way of saying "ready...set...GO!" The arrangement of *Old Time Religion* below not only gives you practice on slides, it also demonstrates pickup notes. Usually rests will appear in the last partial measure, so all beats are accounted for the final repetition of the song. However, when repeating the song ignore the rests. Proceed directly from the last note in the last measure to the first pickup note.

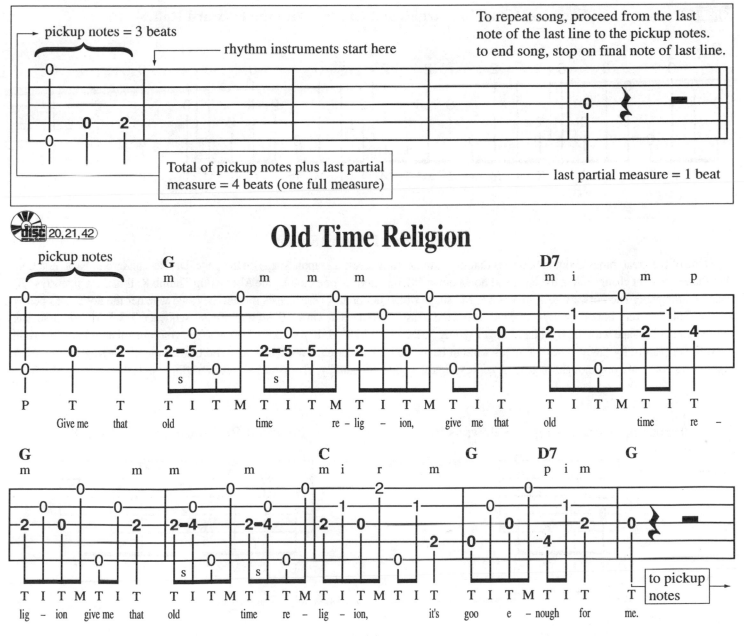

Old Time Religion

Lesson 9 – The Forward Roll

There are several rolls which form the musical "vocabulary" of banjo players. One of the most useful is the Forward Roll. The *Forward Roll* can loosely be defined as any roll which features a **T I M** right hand sequence as the predominant pattern. Listen to the eight-note forward roll below on the recording, then play it over and over until you can talk while doing it without making any errors. Practice emphasizing the first note. This makes the melody obvious in songs and helps you keep your place when playing at faster speeds. It's like a marker note...after you have mastered the roll, do not focus on the individual notes. Focus only on the first note of each roll. The other notes will be played almost unconsciously. Your speed will increase more quickly because with one thought you are playing eight notes.

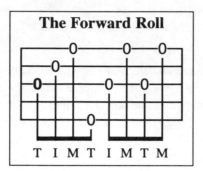

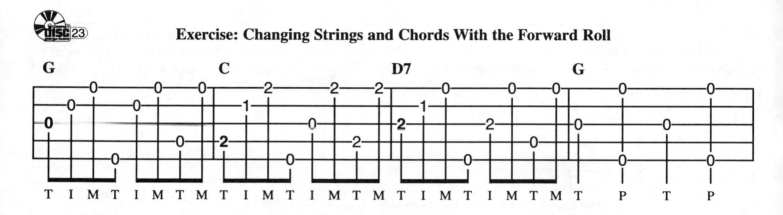

Exercise: Changing Strings and Chords With the Forward Roll

Recognizing Rolls by Shape

One of the great things about tablature is that the different rolls create a graphic shape on the page. Unlike standard musical notation, this shape does not change when the left hand holds down different notes. For example, the Alternating Thumb Roll make a sideways "Z" shape on the page. The Forward Roll makes an "M" shape with a tail on it. These shapes remain the same whether the notes are open or fretted. This is a very important aspect of tab. You learn to associate the sideways "Z" with the finger sequence **T I T M.** You associate the "M and tail" shape with the right hand finger sequence **T I M T I M T M.** If you recognize the shape you immediately know the right hand finger pattern for the next several notes without having to look under each note. In a very short time you are playing four notes or eight notes with only one thought instead of addressing each note individually. This is one secret to reading tab faster.

Alternating Thumb shape: Sideways "Z"

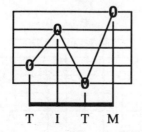

Forward Roll shape: "M with tail"

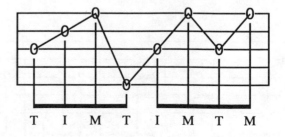

Licks

We call a right and left hand combination that produces a melody fragment a "lick". The fluent tab reader will recognize a common "lick" as a larger segment of music instead of random individual notes. It is like reading text. You do not read the alphabet letters, your mind sees the common combinations of alphabet letters and immediately the word created by these letters forms in the mind. In learning banjo, you first learn the alphabet (the individual notes) then learn to think in terms of rolls. Finally you make a quantum leap in understanding and start to think in licks. Later you begin to realize these rolls and licks are somewhat interchangeable. They are like musical "building blocks".

In the beginning your songs sound very mechanical. This is partially because you have not developed enough speed to make the melody notes stand out from the fill notes. It is also because you are thinking only of the individual notes as you play them, one at a time. When you start to recognize licks, you begin to think of how the music *sounds* instead of what finger you are using or what fret you are holding. Your playing becomes less mechanical - it starts to breathe. If the tune is fully memorized, you are humming the *sound* of the song to yourself as you play, and others can hear the melody in your playing as well.

Cotton - Eyed Joe

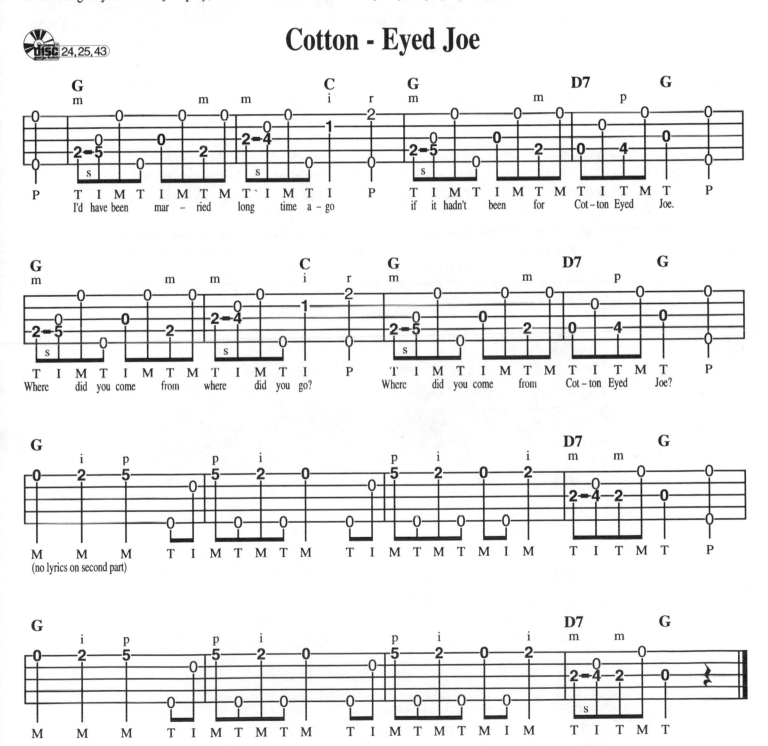

Lesson 10 – The Hammer - On

The *Hammer-on* is a left-hand technique that adds interest and emphasizes melody notes. It is similar to the slide in that it produces two notes, even though the right hand strikes the string only once. The well-executed hammer-on has a "snappier" sound than a slide. In tablature, the hammer-on will be shown as two notes with a dash between them and the letter "h" underneath. To perform a hammer-on, play the first note of the hammer-on with the right hand finger and snap the left hand finger down on the second note immediately afterwards. If the finger is snapped down briskly enough, the second note will be heard without the right hand finger ever striking the string.

Unlike most slides, the second note of the hammer-on will usually occur before the following fill note. In order to show this in tablature, we will introduce the *sixteenth note*. It lasts a sixteenth of a measure, or half the duration of an eighth note. The sixteenth note will be indicated by a double beam.

Unlike the slide, the hammer-on can be performed from an open string to a fretted note. It is also possible to hammer-on from a fretted note to another fretted note. Due to the nature of the maneuver, the second note will always be higher in pitch (up the fingerboard) than the first note. When performing a hammer-on from a fretted note to an adjacent fretted note, the index finger of the left hand is commonly used for the first note. For the second note, use either the middle finger or ring finger, whichever moves more freely. The most common hammer-ons are shown below.

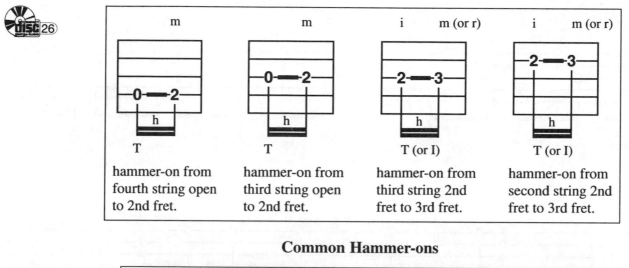

Common Hammer-ons

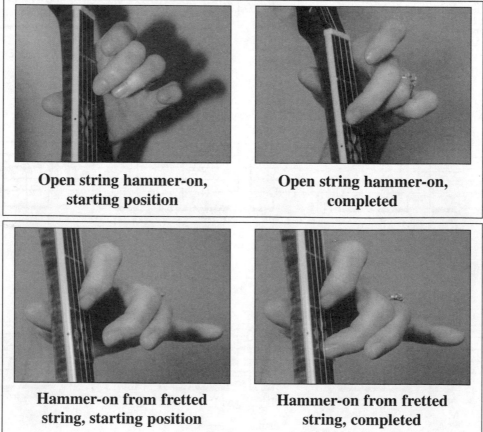

Open string hammer-on, starting position

Open string hammer-on, completed

Hammer-on from fretted string, starting position

Hammer-on from fretted string, completed

Exercise: The Hammer-on with Rolls

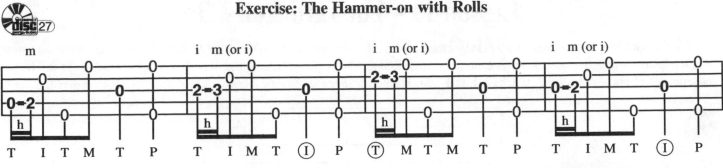

The E Minor Chord

There are several different types of chords. The most common are Major, minor and seventh chords. We have already learned the most common Major and seventh chords in the key of G major. Now we will learn the *Em* chord, the most common minor chord in the key of G major. An easy way to learn the Em chord is to form a C chord and simply remove the index finger.

Caution Marks

Sometimes when concentrating on performing a left hand maneuver, the right hand will make a mistake. Common right hand mistakes include:

a) Using the Index finger on a second string melody note when the tab calls for the thumb.
b) Using the thumb on the note immediately following a fifth string eighth note. (Remember, *never* use the same finger on a note following an eighth note.)

In the following arrangements notice the right hand fingering symbol circled in potential problem spots. Be sure to use the right hand finger indicated by this *Caution Mark.*

Repeat Marks

To eliminate wasted space on the page, *Repeat Marks* are sometimes used when an entire section of music is to be repeated exactly. A repeat mark consists of a heavy vertical line with two dots next to it. If there is a single repeat mark, repeat back to the beginning. If the repeat marks appear as a set (like brackets or parentheses) repeat only the material within the set of repeat marks then proceed.

Cumberland Gap

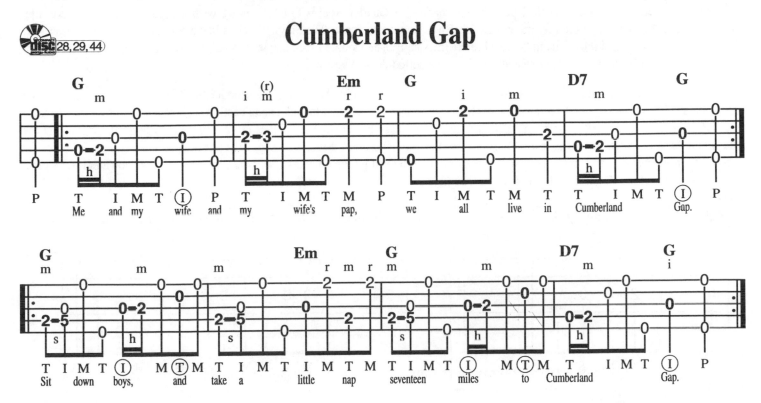

27

Lesson 11 – Forward Roll # 2

The Forward Roll shown in Lesson 9 is very useful because it places the stronger Thumb on the beats of "one" and "four", the most common beats for melody notes. There is another Forward Roll that banjo players like to use. We will call it Forward Roll # 2. The finger sequence of Forward Roll # 2 is: **T M T I M T I M.** Practice the Forward Roll #2 a few thousand times and then proceed.

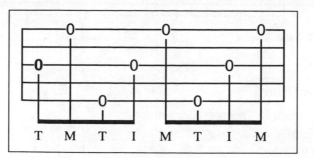

Reminder - Recognizing Roll Shapes

Remember to notice the shape of the rolls. If a line is drawn through the notes, the Alternating Thumb roll (**T I T M**) forms a sideways "Z" shape. Forward Roll # 1 (**T I M T I M T M**) forms an "M" shape with a "tail" on the end. Forward Roll #2 (**T M T I M T I M**) forms a "W" shape with a "nose" in the front. Remember, recognizing the rolls by shape will speed your tab reading because it will help you choose the proper right hand fingers without having to look below every single note.

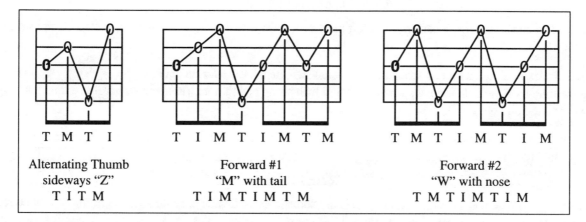

Alternating Thumb	Forward #1	Forward #2
sideways "Z"	"M" with tail	"W" with nose
T I T M	T I M T I M T M	T M T I M T I M

The Tag Lick

Remember learning about "musical punctuation marks"? A Quarter Note is to banjo music what a capital letter is to the written word. It means this word is more important than other words in the sentence. The Single Pinch is like a comma. It separates ideas within a musical sentence and allows us to "take a breath" musically. The Double Pinch has more finality, like a period at the end of a sentence. It signals the completion of a musical idea just as a period does in writing.

However, we need a musical punctuation mark with even more finality. We will now introduce the *Tag Lick*. Like a Double Pinch, it can be used to signal the end of a musical sentence, but it may also be used to end a song section such as a verse or chorus. Practice the Tag Lick below. You may wish to go back and insert it in place of the Double Pinches in your previously learned songs. Note that the first note of the Tag Lick is the last melody note of the musical phrase. It will almost always be the open third string, a G note. The Tag Lick only consumes five beats, so it will commonly be followed by three beats of fill notes, either a roll (as shown below) a pinch or pickup notes taking the listener to the first melody note of the next phrase.

The Tag Lick

Exercise: The Tag Lick with Roll Fill Notes

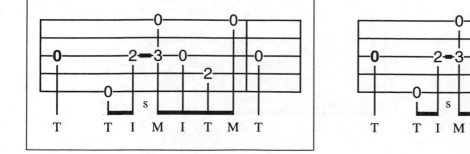

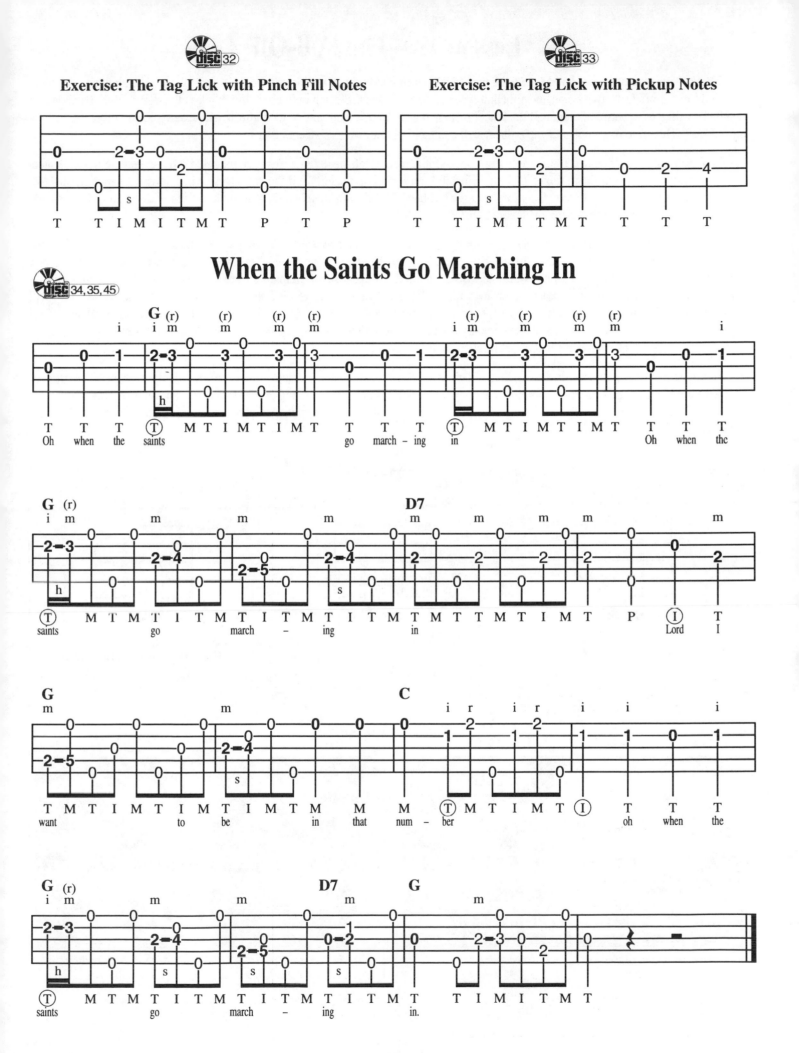

Exercise: The Tag Lick with Pinch Fill Notes

Exercise: The Tag Lick with Pickup Notes

When the Saints Go Marching In

Lesson 12 – The Pull-Off

The *Pull-off* is another left-hand technique that adds interest and emphasizes melody notes. It is similar to the slide and the hammer-on in that it produces two notes, even though the right hand strikes the string only once. In tablature, the pull-off will be shown as two notes with a dash between them and the letter "p" underneath. The second note of the pull-off will usually occur before the following fill note. Therefore, both notes of the pull-off will commonly be shown as sixteenth notes.

To perform a pull-off from a fretted note to an open string, place a left-hand finger (usually the middle finger) on the fret indicated. Pick the string with the right-hand finger, then immediately afterward snap the left hand finger to the side in a downward motion (towards the floor). You are actually "picking" the string with the left-hand finger, immediately after striking the string with the right-hand finger. Pull-offs from the second fret are the most common.

To perform a pull-off from a fretted string to another fretted string, place two left-hand fingers on adjacent frets as indicated by the tab. Pick the string with the right-hand finger, then "snap" the left-hand finger on the higher note to the side in a downward motion (towards the floor). The finger on the lower note (usually the index finger) should remain on the fret until after the following note is played. Again, you are actually picking the string with the left-hand finger. Due to the nature of the maneuver, the second note will always be lower in pitch (down the fingerboard) than the first note. When performing a pull-off from a fretted note to an adjacent fretted note, the index finger of the left hand is commonly used for the lower (second) note. Either the middle finger or ring finger, whichever moves more freely, can be used for the first (higher) note.

The most common pull-offs are shown below. This is a difficult maneuver, so practice the exercise diligently before attempting to use the pull-off in a song. Remember, none of the left hand maneuvers change the timing of the right hand. The note spacing of the right hand remains uniform even though the left hand is producing a note that occurs in between notes that are produced solely by the right hand fingers.

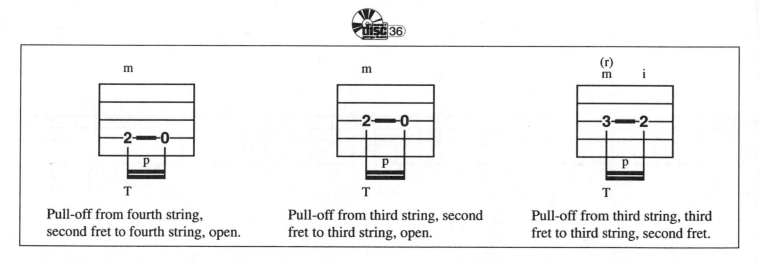

Pull-off from fourth string, second fret to fourth string, open.

Pull-off from third string, second fret to third string, open.

Pull-off from third string, third fret to third string, second fret.

Common Pull-offs

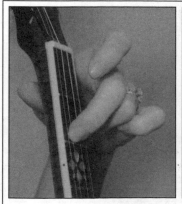

Open string pull-off, starting position

Open string pull-off, completed

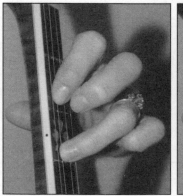

Fretted string pull-off, starting position

Fretted string pull-off, completed

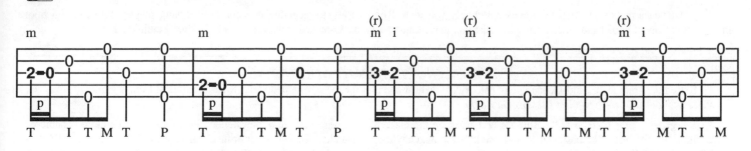

In *Cripple Creek* below, the 2-5 slides on the first string consume *two full beats*. The first string/fifth fret note at the end of the slide is not played with the right hand. It is generated totally from the slide maneuver.

Cripple Creek

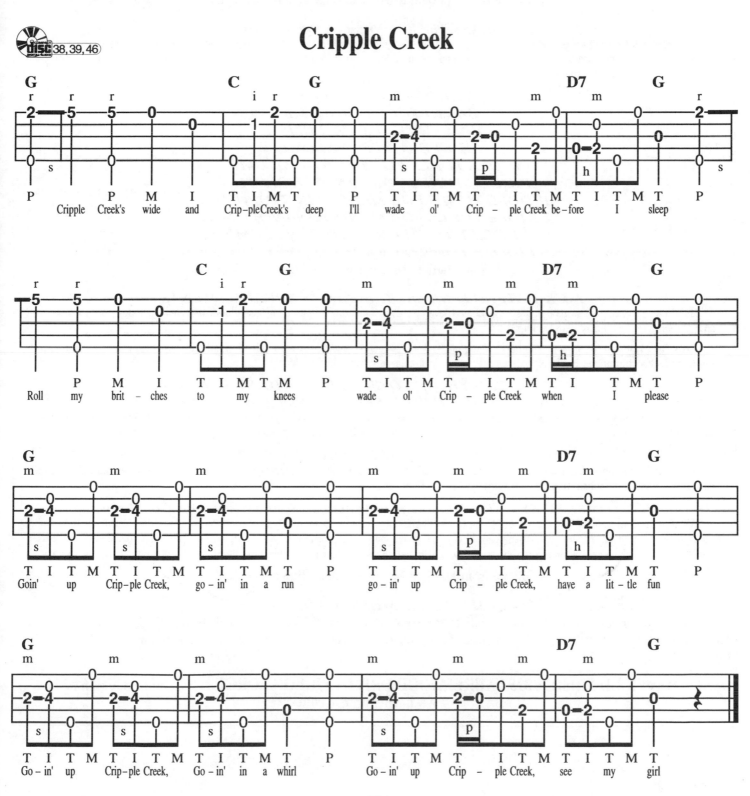

For Further Study...

If you have learned the lessons in this book thoroughly, you are well on your way to becoming an accomplished banjo player. Mel Bay Publications, Inc. offers dozens of books and videos that will assist you in continuing your banjo-related endeavors. Books by Jack Hatfield are listed.

BLUEGRASS BANJO METHOD

Extremely graduated. Bold-faced melody notes help you hear and play the melody immediately. Takes the student from beginner to advanced level. Excellent follow-up to *First Lessons On Banjo*.

Bluegrass Banjo Method is "...Still the best book on the market for beginners."-Banjo Newsletter , Feb. 1994. "...It's more capable of {teaching the beginner} the basics of Scruggs style banjo than any other manual..." Bluegrass Unlimited, January 1985. *BLUEGRASS BANJO METHOD, BOOK 2*-Playing in 3/4 time, Up the Neck, Different Keys, Learning the Fingerboard. Both levels include demo recording with banjo on one channel, rhythm instruments on the other.

Available from Hatfield Music and other fine music dealers.

GRASS TRAX™ Practice Recordings

Guitar, mandolin and bass play rhythm to the most popular bluegrass instrumentals. Rhythm instruments are in one channel, lead in the other. All songs are played at learning speed and at performing speed. Tablature included for banjo, guitar, fiddle and mandolin. Ten tunes on each recording. Ten recordings available:

BANJO TUNES - VOLUME 1
BANJO TUNES - VOLUME 2
FIDDLE TUNES - VOLUME 1
FIDDLE TUNES - VOLUME 2
FIDDLE TUNES FOR BANJO - VOLUME 1
FIDDLE TUNES FOR BANJO - VOLUME 2
FIDDLE TUNES FOR MANDOLIN - VOLUME 1
FIDDLE TUNES FOR MANDOLIN - VOLUME 2
FIDDLE TUNES FOR GUITAR - VOLUME 1
FIDDLE TUNES FOR GUITAR - VOLUME 2

Available from Hatfield Music and other fine music dealers.

JACK HATFIELD BANJO TABLATURE ARRANGEMENTS

Hundreds of arrangements, beginner to advanced level. Scruggs, melodic, single-string and classical styles. Includes note-for-note Earl Scruggs transcriptions, many with backup.

Also, Jack Hatfield's Beginner's Corner Collections, Gospel Collection, and Christmas Collection, all with slow/fast recording and reprints from from Jack's columns in Banjo Newsletter magazine. Available only from Hatfield Music.

YOU CAN TEACH YOURSELF® BANJO BY EAR
YOU CAN TEACH YOURSELF® MANDOLIN BY EAR

Learn how to play chord progressions and melodies by ear, "fake" a solo, create a melody-oriented solo, and use licks to fake a solo or embellish the melody-oriented solo. Includes demonstration C.D. recording. Mel Bay Publications, Inc.

OLD-TIME GOSPEL BANJO SOLOS®

Banjo tablature, musical notation, and lyrics to thirty of the most-loved gospel songs, arranged from beginner to advanced, including up-the-neck solos. Includes demonstration C.D. recording. Mel Bay Publications.

HOW TO PLAY BY EAR - A Guide for Musicians, Songwriters, and Composers.

Written for all musicians, any instrument. Great for songwriters and those who are overly dependent on notation or tab. Explains: the number system, scales, chord construction, identifying chords by ear, popular song form, probabilities and a step-by-step procedure that simplifies the trial-and-error process. Many ear training exercises on recording which train the ear to hear intervals, bass lines, chord types and chord progressions.

Available from Hatfield Music and other fine music dealers.

HATFIELD MUSIC CATALOG

In-depth descriptions and prices of all Hatfield Music publications plus books by other authors, word books, banjo accessories, instructional videos, digital recorders, and practice aids. Authorized dealer for many major banjo manufacturers. Send S.A.S.E.for free catalog.

HATFIELD MUSIC • 325 LAURELWOOD DRIVE • PIGEON FORGE, TN 37863 • 800-426-8744
www.hatfieldmusic.com